First published in 2025 by Flying Eye Books Ltd.
27 Westgate Street, London, E8 3RL.

Text and illustrations © Ella Bailey 2025.
Ella Bailey has asserted her right under the Copyright, Designs and
Patents Act, 1988, to be identified as the Author and Illustrator of this Work.

All rights reserved. No part of this publication may be reproduced or transmitted in any form
or by any means, electronic or mechanical, including photocopying, recording or by any
information and storage retrieval system, without prior written consent from the publisher.

Edited by Sara Forster & Maryam Elahi
Designed by Riko Sekiguchi & Maisy Ruffels

Consultant: Dr. Matthew Dempsey

1 3 5 7 9 10 8 6 4 2

Published in the US by Flying Eye Books Ltd.
Printed in China on FSC® certified paper.

ISBN: 978-1-83874-212-6
US Library Edition ISBN: 978-1-83874-932-3
www.flyingeyebooks.com

ELLA BAILEY

ONE DAY ON OUR PREHISTORIC PLANET

...WITH A T.REX

FLYING EYE BOOKS

As the sun rises over a prehistoric land, a little *Tyrannosaurus rex* darts across lands of flowers and ferns.

There is his brother,

and his sister,

and over here . . .

. . . Is their mother!

She may be a predator, with a powerful jaw full of long, sharp teeth, but she is very gentle with her babies.

Since they hatched from their eggs, they have gone everywhere with their mother.

The siblings follow their mother as she leads them through the lush forest they call home.

Along the bank of a wide, winding river where strange creatures swim . . .

The tiny carnivore scurries to keep up with his mother. He must run very fast because each one of her steps is equal to many of his!

He copies his mother as she raises her huge head into the air.

Her powerful nose has caught the scent of something tasty...

time to investigate!

Uh-oh! This meal is already taken.

The only animal that could chase away a T. rex, is another T. rex!

Today, their mother will have to hunt for their dinner.

One day, the young Tyrannosaurus and his siblings will be able to fend for themselves,

but for now their mother will take good care of them.

With full tummies, the small family curl up together to sleep away the rest of the warm night . . .

. . . Until the sun rises on another day on our prehistoric planet, long, long ago.